# Mind Your Language 4

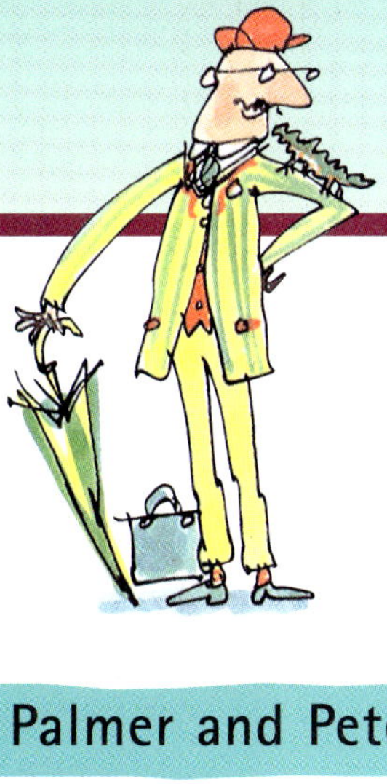

by Sue Palmer and Peter Brinton

## Acknowledgements

We are grateful to the following for giving permission to reproduce extracts from copyright works: Grafton Books, a Division of the Collins Publishing group for 'in Just-spring' by e. e. cummings from *The Complete Poems 1913-1962*; 'Biffo the Bear' extract copyright © D.C. Thompson & Co. Ltd, 1985. Reprinted by permission D.C. Thompson & Co. Ltd; A.P. Watt Ltd, on behalf of Richard Ashbee from *William and the Space Animal* by Richmal Crompton.

Every effort has been made to contact copyright holders, but in some cases it has been impossible to do so. We apologise for any infringement that may have inadvertently occurred.

Addison Wesley Longman Limited
Edinburgh Gate, Harlow, Essex, CM20 2JE, England
and Associated Companies throughout the world.

All rights reserved: no part of this publication may be reproduced, stored in a retrieval system, or transmitted in any form or by any means electronic, mechanical, photocopying, recording, or otherwise without either the prior written permission of the Publishers or a licence permitting restricted copying in the United Kingdom issued by the Copyright Licensing Agency Ltd, 90 Tottenham Court Road, London, W1P 9HE.

First edition published 1988

This edition published 1998
ISBN 0582 319501

Produced by Addison Wesley Longman Singapore Pte Ltd
Printed in Singapore

The publisher's policy is to use paper manufactured from sustainable forests.

# Contents

*Chapter 1*
Parts of Speech: Nouns, Verbs, Pronouns, Adjectives and Adverbs ............ 4

*Chapter 2*
Punctuation (Including Brackets and Dashes) ............ 10

*Chapter 3*
Capital Letters ............ 18

*Chapter 4*
Subjects, Verbs and Objects ............ 26

*Chapter 5*
Spoken and Written Language: Standard English ............ 32

*Chapter 6*
The Apostrophe to show Ownership ............ 38

*Chapter 7*
Words at Work: Adverbs, Prepositions and Conjunctions ............ 44

*Chapter 8*
Inverted Commas ............ 51

*Chapter 9*
Words and Meaning: Idioms ............ 57

*Chapter 10*
Active and Passive Sentences ............ 60

*Chapter 11*
Sorts of Sentences and Sentence Transformations ............ 67

# Parts of Speech: Nouns, Verbs, Pronouns, Adjectives and Adverbs

Match the parts of speech with the correct definitions.

- tells you more about how, when or where something happened
- name of a person, place or thing
- stands in place of a noun
- word that tells you what's happening
- describes a noun

Noun   Adjective   Adverb   Verb   Pronoun

In this silly poem some words are underlined. They are all the same part of speech. What part of speech is it?

Nobody <u>likes</u> me, everybody hates me,

<u>I'm</u> going outside <u>to eat</u> worms –

Short fat juicy ones, long thin squooshy ones,

<u>See</u> how they <u>squiggle</u> and squirm!

<u>Chop</u> off the heads and suck out the juice

And throw their skins away –

Nobody <u>knows</u> how much I <u>thrive</u>
On worms three times a day.

There are *four* more examples of the same part of speech in the poem. Find them all.

The next silly poem is a version of a nursery rhyme. Some of the words have a wiggly line underneath. They are all the same part of speech – what is it?

> Little Miss Muffet
> Sat on a tuffet,
> Eating an Irish stew.
> There came a big spider
> Who sat down beside her –
> So Little Miss M ate him too.

There are *two* more examples of the same part of speech in the poem. Find them both.

In this last rhyme, some of the words have a ring round them. Again, all the ringed words are the same part of speech. What part of speech is it?

> I eat my peas with honey –
> I've done it all my life.
> It makes the peas taste funny,
> But it keeps them on my knife.

There are five more examples of that part of speech in the poem. Find them all.

**Parts of Speech Race**

Work in pairs. You will need some scrap paper, and your teacher will need a stop watch or a watch which indicates seconds.

When you are given the command GO, you have to find:

> Four different pronouns in
>    Nobody Likes Me;
> Four different verbs in
>    Little Miss Muffet;
> Three different nouns in
>    I Eat My Peas With Honey.

As soon as you have collected all eleven words, put your hand up to get your time. Make a note of it on your paper.

When the class is ready, your teacher can check to find which pair got all eleven words right in the shortest time.

5

## Adjectives and Adverbs

Both adjectives and adverbs give added detail. Which of them tell you more about a noun? Which of them tell you more about a verb?

In this sentence, find *three adjectives* and *one adverb of manner* (answering the question "how?"):

> The sly old fox crept stealthily into the silent farmyard.

How would the sentence read if you took all the adjectives and adverbs out?

By removing adjectives and adverbs, you can reduce a sentence to its bare bones. This is called *reduction*.

In this sentence, find *three adjectives*, and *two adverbs of time* (answering the question "when?")

> Nowadays, young people often wear blue denim jeans.

How would the sentence read if you took out the adjectives and adverbs?

Reduce this sentence by taking out: *one adjective, one adverb of time, one adverb of manner* and *one adverb of place* (answering the question "where"?)

> Yesterday the old bear upstairs was sleeping soundly.

Which part of speech is each of the words you have taken out?
How many adjectives can you find in the third line of the poem *Nobody Likes Me*? (page 4)
What would that line reduce to if you took out the adjectives?

How many adverbs can you find in this poem from *Alice in Wonderland*? What are they, and what does the poem sound like without them?

> Speak roughly to your little boy,
> And beat him when he sneezes:
> He only does it to annoy,
> Because he knows it teases.
>
> I speak severely to my boy,
> And beat him when he sneezes:
> For he can thoroughly enjoy
> The pepper when he pleases.
>
> *Lewis Carroll*

*Grow your own sentences*

Work with a partner. In the box below are three short sentences. They have all been reduced so they have no adverbs or adjectives in them at all.

1) The leopard raced across the plain.
2) A girl bought the dog.
3) The teacher drank his coffee.

Choose one of these sentences and copy it out neatly on to a strip of paper. Cut the sentence up into individual words. Then think of two adjectives and two adverbs that would fit well into the sentence. Write them on slips of paper too.

How many *different* sentences can you make by putting the adjectives and adverbs into different places in the original sentence? (You are not allowed to change the order of the original sentence at all.) Keep a note of each expanded sentence that you make. At the end, your teacher may let some people tell their sentences to the class. Which pair can get the most?

**In your language book**

Write the heading: **Parts of Speech**

**A** Copy and complete:

> Words have different jobs to do in a sentence. The sort of job a word does depends on what p_____ of s_____ it is.
> A noun is _____.
> A verb is _____.
> An adjective _____.
> An adverb _____.
> A pronoun _____.

**B** Copy out two of the poems on pages 4 and 5 and mark all the verbs (by underlining them), all the nouns (by putting wiggly lines under them) and all the pronouns (by putting rings round them).

**C**

> There was an old man of Darjeeling –
> He travelled from London to Ealing.
> It said on the door,
> "Please don't spit on the floor,"
> So he carefully spat on the ceiling.

Copy out this limerick, leaving yourself plenty of space to mark the following:

Underline five verbs.

Put a wiggly line under seven nouns.

Put rings round three pronouns.

Put a box round one adjective.

Put arrows underneath to show one adverb.

**D** Reduce the following sentences by taking out all the adjectives and adverbs. Write down the reduced sentences.

1) Slowly, wearily, the little girl climbed the steep hill.
2) A tall handsome man strode purposefully into the empty room.
3) Sometimes a sleek elegant horse jumps clumsily.
4) Modern scientists often work in smart, well-equipped laboratories.
5) The big bad wolf jumped suddenly at the unsuspecting little girl.

**E** 1) Make up a sentence with a lot of adjectives and adverbs in it. Write it in your language book and give it to a friend to reduce. Your friend should write the reduced sentence underneath and sign it, to show whose work it is!
2) Make up a "reduced" sentence with *no* adjectives or adverbs in it. Write it in your language book and give it to a friend to expand. Your friend should expand it by adding some suitable adjectives and adverbs, and writing the expanded sentence underneath. Get your friend to sign it again.

### Record-Breaker!

The English word with the most possible meanings and uses is SET.
It can be used in lots of different ways as a *noun*, a *verb* and an *adjective*. How many can you think of?

### Adjective Poem

This clever little poem called *The Seasons* uses just four nouns and twelve adjectives to get its message across.

SPRING: showery, flowery, bowery;
SUMMER: hoppy, croppy, poppy;
AUTUMN: slippy, drippy, nippy;
WINTER: wheezy, sneezy, freezy.

Why not try your own adjective poem on the days of the week?
MONDAY – mopey, dopey, ropey;
TUESDAY ....

# 2 Punctuation (Including Brackets and Dashes)

In the earlier books of *Mind Your Language* we have seen that punctuation marks in writing can show the tone of voice in which words should be spoken out loud.

What are these two punctuation marks called? What tones of voice could each of them show?

Give some examples of phrases or sentences which would need  when written down.

Now give examples of phrases or sentences which would need !

Punctuation can also show how words should be grouped together to make sense. A full stop shows the end of a sentence – and a sentence should make complete sense on its own. If full stops are missed out, a reader cannot tell how the writer intended a piece to be read:

> Cinderella entered the room on her hands diamond rings glittered on her head a rich tiara sparkled among the golden curls on her pretty little feet two glass slippers gleamed as she swirled through the room in a beautiful silken gown Prince Charming strode towards her

If full stops are put in the wrong places it can turn a passage into gibberish:

> Cinderella. Entered the room on her. Hands diamond rings glittered on. Her head a rich tiara sparkled among. The golden curls on her pretty. Little feet two glass slippers gleamed as she swirled. Through the room in a beautiful silken. Gown Prince Charming strode towards. Her.

Sometimes putting full stops in the wrong places can make a passage seem rather silly:

> Cinderella entered the room on her hands. Diamond rings glittered on her head. A rich tiara sparkled among the golden curls on her pretty little feet. Two glass slippers gleamed as she swirled through the room. In a beautiful silken gown Prince Charming strode towards her.

Can you work out where the full stops *should* come in the above passage to make it read sensibly?

Commas show short breaks *within* sentences. Again, if commas are put in the wrong places it can change the meaning of a piece of writing. Do you remember this example from Book Two?

The monster liked to eat silver paper, gold candlesticks, leather boots and old socks.

The monster liked to eat silver, paper, gold, candlesticks, leather, boots and old socks.

How do the positions of the commas affect the meaning in each case?

How about these examples? Let someone try reading each pair of sentences aloud to show how the position of the commas changes the meaning.

1) The girl had huge, bright blue eyes.
   The girl had huge, bright, blue eyes.

2) I like Mike, who plays the guitar, better than Steve.
   I like Mike, who plays the guitar better than Steve.

3) Napoleon, claimed his enemies, wanted to take over Europe.
   Napoleon claimed his enemies wanted to take over Europe.

How much difference do the commas make in each case?

## Brackets and Dashes

Sometimes you will see brackets used in writing.
1) The old man (who was really the prince) smiled at the princess.

2) Sally spent all her pocket money on horse-riding (she's mad about horses at the moment) but I saved most of mine for the holidays.

3) St Paul's Cathedral was rebuilt in the late seventeenth century to a design by Sir Christopher Wren (the original cathedral had been destroyed in the Great Fire of London, 1666).

4) Common amphibians (animals which live partly on land, partly in water) are frogs, toads and newts.

From the examples above, can you work out how and when brackets are used?

> Another name for brackets is *parenthesis*. The words in brackets are said to be *in parenthesis*. When you've decided on an explanation for the use of brackets, try looking up *parenthesis* in a dictionary to see if you are right.

Sometimes pairs of dashes are used instead of brackets to show parenthesis. A dash is a short horizontal line.
1) The old man – who was really the prince – smiled at the princess.

2) Common amphibians – animals which live partly on land and partly in water – are frogs, toads and newts.

The dash is a versatile punctuation mark – a single dash can also be used instead of a comma or a full stop. It is half-way between the two – stronger than a comma but not as strong as a full stop. It's stronger than a comma because the reader has to make a definite break in his reading when he comes to a dash. But it is not quite as powerful as a full stop – you do not need a capital letter after a dash.

   Often if you can't decide between a comma and a full stop, a dash is the best punctuation mark to use. However, you should not overdo the use of dashes in formal writing. Use as many as you like in informal letters and notes, but try to avoid them in more formal writing tasks.

Dashes have been used frequently in the following sentences. In each case other punctuation marks could have been used instead.

Which of these punctuation marks ( ) . , would you use to replace each of the dashes in the examples? Explain your choice each time.

1) A sandwich – two pieces of bread with a filling inside – takes its name from the Earl of Sandwich, who needed a convenient snack to take with him to race meetings.

2) Sir Robert Peel began the police force in the early nineteenth century – and policemen are sometimes called *bobbies*, because Bob is a short form of Robert.

3) The Earl of Cardigan gave another word to our language – he used to wear knitted woollen jackets, which became known as *cardigans*.

4) Lots of household items are called after their inventors – including *biros*, *hoovers* and *mackintoshes*.

1) Work in teams of about six. You will need paper, pencils and coloured pens.
2) Each team member should choose a short passage from a book, magazine or newspaper – DO *NOT* CHOOSE A PASSAGE WHICH INVOLVES DIRECT SPEECH. Copy out the passages neatly on to paper – *but miss out all the punctuation*.
3) You have about ten minutes in which to write, so don't waste time.
4) At the end of ten minutes, collect all the team's papers together and swap with another team.
5) You now have another ten minutes in which to punctuate all the other team's passages correctly – without looking at the books/magazines they came from! Use coloured pens to put in full stops, capital letters, commas, dashes, brackets, question marks, exclamation marks, apostrophes.

Share out the work to start with, then get together to discuss the punctuation of each passage to make sure it makes good sense.

**Scoring**

Your teacher is the best person to work out the scores. He/she will know whether the punctuation you have chosen is acceptable – it doesn't have to be exactly the same as the original, as long as it makes good sense.

Perhaps your teacher can score the test match while you are doing the exercises at the end of the chapter, and can award points to the teams for their punctuation skills.

**In your language book**

Write the heading: *Punctuation*

**A** Copy and complete:

> Punctuation can show the t_____ of voice in which words would be spoken. A qu_____ m_____ shows a qu_____. An ex_____ m_____ shows a raised voice, or that the words are not to be taken seriously.
>
> Punctuation also shows how words should be grouped to make sense – f_____ st_____s show the ends of sentences, c_____s show smaller breaks within sentences.
>
> B_____s show that words are in parenthesis (aside or separate from the main sentence), and d_____s can be used instead of brackets.
>
> A single d_____ can show a break half-way between a c_____ and a f_____ st_____, but the d_____ should not be used too often.

**B** Copy out this passage, putting in *full stops*, *commas* and *capital letters* so that it makes sense.

> Our sun is a star this means that it is a sphere of burning gases the other stars we see at night are spheres of burning gases too they look smaller than the sun because they are much much further away the sun is only 93 million miles away from the earth it gives our planet the light and heat we need for life to exist here.

**C** Copy out these sentences, putting commas in where necessary to improve the sense.

> 1) The three sections of our local library are fiction non-fiction and reference.
> 2) Reference books must never be taken out of the library but fiction and non-fiction books can be borrowed and taken home.
> 3) Non-fiction which means fact is arranged in subject groups such as history geography science and hobbies.
> 4) Fiction books are story books and are arranged on the shelves in alphabetical order of authors' names starting at A and going on to Z.

**D** Copy out sentences 1–4 on page 14, putting commas, full stops or brackets in place of the dashes. Make sure you choose the most suitable punctuation mark in each case.

**E** 1) Make up and write in your book a sentence involving the use of brackets to show parenthesis.
2) Write the same sentence, using dashes instead of brackets.
3) Make up and write a sentence involving a single dash.
4) Write the same sentence, using a comma or full stop in place of the dash (whichever is more suitable).

**F** Look back over some of your own recent written work (a story or some project work). Is your punctuation as good as it could be? Pretend to be a teacher and improve the punctuation so that your writing makes better sense.

# Capital Letters

**A B C D E F G H I J K L M
N O P Q R S T U V W X Y Z**

in the first three books of *mind your language* we have already looked at capital letters many times. you should be able to tell your teacher where capital letters are missing in this passage. altogether there are six missing capitals.

You should know by now that capital letters are needed at the *beginnings of sentences* and for *proper nouns* (the special names of particular people, places or things).

**Hunt the Proper Noun**

There are many types of proper noun. The most obvious are the *forenames* and *surnames of people* (e.g. Florence Nightingale) and *names of towns and cities* (e.g. London). But there are also *days of the week* (e.g. Tuesday), *film titles* (e.g. *Lady and the Tramp*) and many more.

In the following sentences we have included lots of proper nouns – you can spot them by the capital letters. With a partner, you are going to join in a race to list as many different sorts of proper noun as you can. Your teacher will give you ten minutes. In that time, try to find more **types of proper noun** than any other pair in the class – note them down on scrap paper like this:

*countries, towns, nationalities*

1) Christmas Day and Easter Sunday are religious festivals.

2) Judy Blume is an American novelist. One of her best books is called *Tales of a Fourth Grade Nothing*.

3) Some of my favourite television programmes are Top of the Pops, Blue Peter and Grange Hill.

4) The Prime Minister visits Buckingham Palace every Tuesday.

5) We start our holiday on Thursday, 14th April.

6) When I was in London I went to Wembley Stadium.

7) Have you ever seen Tower Bridge over the River Thames?

8) On our bicycle trip we visited Truro and St Austell.

9) The English cricket team visited the West Indies.

10) West Bromwich Albion might win the Football Association Cup this season.

11) Our local supermarket sells many types of washing powder – Bold, Persil, Surf, Omo and Ariel are just a few.

12) I think the shop you want is on Lemon Street.

13) Matthew took Towser for a walk in Albert Park.

(You may think of some other types that we have not included.) The winners are the pair who list the most types of proper noun, as approved by your teacher.

There are other times when capital letters are used. Look at these examples and try to name *four* other occasions when capital letters are required.

### Example One

A centipede was happy quite,
Until a frog in fun
Said, "Pray, which leg comes after which?"
This raised her mind to such a pitch,
She lay distracted in the ditch
Considering how to run.

*Anon.*

'Tis dogs' delight to bark and bite,
And little birds to sing,
But if you sit on a red-hot brick
It's the sign of an early spring.

*Anon.*

### Example Two

There was a discussion programme on BBC last night. On the panel were the leader of the TUC, a representative of the NUM, Mr Roy Barker, QC, and a Conservative MP. They discussed the peace talks between the USA and the USSR, and whether the EEC should be involved. I got fed up and turned over to ITV to watch a programme about the FA Cup.

### Example Three

I woke up to find the sun streaming in through my bedroom window. When I had washed and dressed, I went downstairs to cook my breakfast. What a surprise I had! The living room was completely wrecked – I had been burgled! What should I do?

Quickly I went to the telephone and dialled 999. A panda car was sent round to my house straight away, and I opened the door to a detective sergeant, dressed in plain clothes. He questioned me about my belongings and then examined the room for fingerprints.

### Example Four

The Lord's my shepherd, I'll not want.
He makes me down to lie
In pastures green, He leadeth me
The quiet waters by.

My soul He doth restore again;
And me to walk doth make
Within the paths of righteousness,
E'en for His own name's sake.

Yea, though I walk in death's dark vale,
Yet will I fear none ill:
For Thou art with me; and Thy rod
And staff me comfort still.

The answers, if you need to check them out, are on page 25.

## "In the News" Collage

One place where you usually find plenty of abbreviations is in a newspaper.

Work with a partner. You will need a piece of paper, glue and one or more daily newspapers. Look through the papers for examples of abbreviations where capital letters are required, as in our example.

Cut them out neatly and stick them on to your paper to make a collage. Under each one, write what the abbreviations stand for (this would look best in bright colours – use felt tip pens if possible).

Try not to leave too much space between the cut-outs – collages look best if they are quite crowded!

**In your language book**

Write the heading: **Capital Letters**

**A** Copy and complete:

> A c_____ letter should always be used at the b_____ of a sentence, and for the first letter of p_____ nouns. There are many types of proper noun, including _____, _____, _____, _____, and _____. C_____ letters are also required for the pronoun _____, the first letter of each line in a p_____, some a_____s, and words referring to G_____ and other important figures in world religions.

**B** Copy out these sentences, putting in the capital letters where required.

> 1) the postman delivered the letters to orchard road.
> 2) daffodils bloom in the springtime.
> 3) there is a good film showing at the plaza cinema on tuesday.
> 4) hannah said that i had not read the book by roald dahl.
> 5) last august i went to spain for my holiday.

**C** Abbreviations. Copy out these phrases and beside each one write out its abbreviated form.

> Royal Air Force _____
> Her Royal Highness _____
> Prime Minister _____
> Marylebone Cricket Club _____
> Member of Parliament _____
> British Broadcasting Corporation _____
> On Her Majesty's Service _____
> Please Turn Over _____

**D** Copy out these sentences, putting in capital letters where required.

1) the pm lives at no 10 downing street in westminster, which is a part of london.
2) brazil is the largest country in south america. it is even larger than the whole of the usa.
3) a man called bram stoker wrote *dracula*, but *frankenstein* was written by a woman, mary shelley.
4) the eldest son of the king or queen of england is given the title of prince of wales.

**E** In this extract from the TV page of a newspaper all the capital letters have been missed out. Write out the extract, putting in the capital letters.

*television programmes for tuesday 14th march*

**bbc 1**
3.55  up our street
4.10  dogtanian and the three muskehounds
4.35  take two
5.00  newsround
5.05  the flintstones

**itv london**
4.00  portland bill
4.10  the blunders
4.30  scooby doo
4.45  making of the ark
5.15  connections
5.45  news

Here's a poem by the American poet, e.e. cummings, who played about with punctuation and with capital letters. Why do you think he did it? Can you imagine how his poem would look if it was punctuated "correctly"? Would it say the same thing?

## in Just-spring

in Just-
spring when the world is mud-
lucious the little
lame balloonman

whistles   far   and wee

and eddieandbill come
running from marbles and
piracies and it's
spring

when the world is puddle-wonderful

the queer
old balloonman whistles
far   and   wee
and bettyandisbel come dancing

from hop-scotch and jump-rope and

it's
spring
and

   the

        goat-footed

balloonman   whistles
far
and
wee

*e.e. cummings*

### Abbreviations Quiz

At the back of most dictionaries, you will find a list of common abbreviations. When you've got some spare time, try using this to hold a quiz session with your friends. One person can be quizmaster and ask what abbreviations stand for. The others can see who is Champion Abbreviator!

### Answers (page 20)

*Example One*

The first letter of each line of a poem *usually* begins with a capital letter.

(Some modern poets, like e.e. cummings, don't use this convention.)

*Example Two*

Many abbreviations use capital letters (e.g.: TV) but some don't (e.g.: e.g.).

*Example Three*

The pronoun *I* always has a capital – to show how important "I am"!

*Example Four*

Any words referring to God are given a capital – His, He, Thy, and so on. So are words referring to other very holy people, like Jesus and Mohammed.

25

# 4 Subjects, Verbs and Objects

In Book 3 we learned that every clause has a *subject* and a *verb* (or *verb phrase*). The simplest clauses just have a subject and a verb, like this one:

who → **S** The dog **V** growled. ← did what

Some clauses also have an *object*.

**S** Ralph **V** trimmed the **O** sheep.

who · did what · to whom

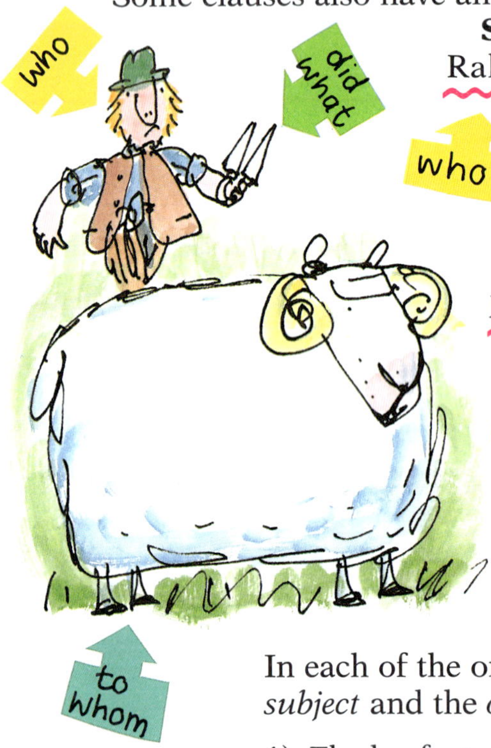


**S** Mr Briggs **V** encouraged **O** Bruce.

who · did what · to whom

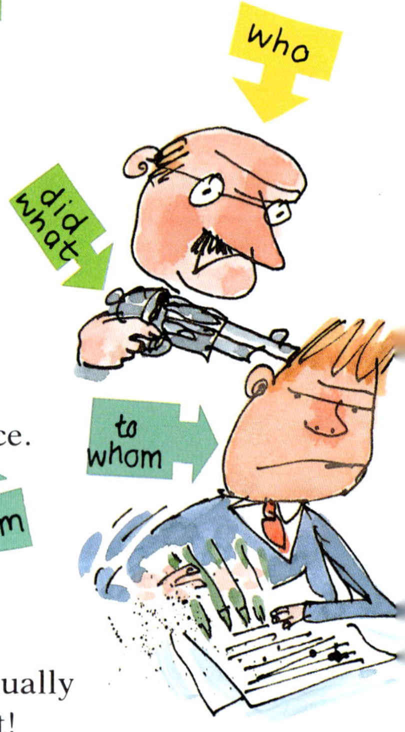


The object of the verb usually has something done to it!

In each of the one-clause sentences below, name the *verb*, the *subject* and the *object*.

1) The beefeater guarded the crown jewels.
2) A handsome prince opened the door.
3) Gently, he kissed the sleeping princess.
4) The Prime Minister read the papers.
5) I like her.
6) Unfortunately, she dislikes me.

In all these examples, where is the *subject* in relation to the *verb*? Where is the *object* in relation to the *verb*?

Expand the *subjects* and *objects* in these sentences into noun phrases:

1) **S V O** He kicks it.
2) **S V O** They love her.
3) **S V O** She hates it.
4) **S V O** It attacked them.

In these sentences reduce the *subjects* and *objects* to *pronouns*:

1) The television announcer read the news bulletin.
2) Sir Francis Drake singed the King of Spain's beard.
3) Florence Nightingale tended the wounded soldier.
4) Saudi Arabia produces a great deal of oil.
5) The children in this class adore their teacher.

All sentences have subjects and verbs, but only *some* sentences have objects.
 Not all verbs take objects. It has to be a certain type of verb (called a transitive verb). There are some transitive verbs below. Use them to make up some SVO sentences of your own (put the verbs into past, present or future tense, as necessary).

**S V O** Our teacher praises us.

**S V O** I like TV.

**S V O** The Queen ate a jam sandwich.

**Transitive Verbs**
to like  to teach
to eat  to scold  to hate
to hit  to attack
to chase  to scratch  to cook
to meet  to praise
to tickle  to kiss

**S V O** My brother chases girls.

**S V O** The Daleks attacked the city.

**S V O** Mrs Barton teaches the infants.

### Silly Gossip

Work in groups of four. You will each need a piece of paper and a pencil.

This game involves writing a subject, a verb, an object, and an adverbial (which is another sentence component, giving extra information about where, when, etc.).

In each case

**the *subject* is a person** → e.g. Popeye the Sailorman   George Michael   The Queen   Charlie Brown   William the Conqueror   Roald Dahl   The President of the U.S.A.   The person who wrote this book

**the *verb* is *transitive*** → See the green bubble opposite

**the *object* can be a person or a thing** → e.g. a red-spotted cow   the King of Spain   Winston Churchill   a large pink jelly   an apple   Sherlock Holmes

**the *adverbial* tells you more about when, where, how or why –** → e.g. on the school field   every Thursday   under the desk   after tea   in the middle of June   at the top of Blackpool tower   with a rose behind his/her ear   at the FA cup final

**Details of how to play are on the next page.**

1) Each person folds his/her piece of paper into four sections, and labels them S, V, O, Adverbial.

S
V
O
Adverbial

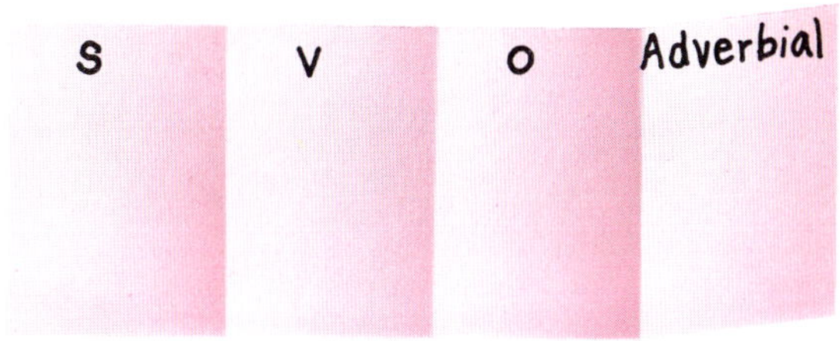

2) In the first section, you write a subject (choose from our examples or make up your own).

S
V
O
Adverbial
The Queen

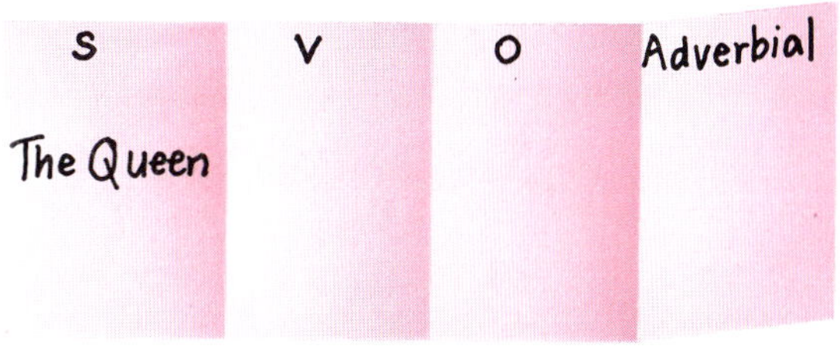

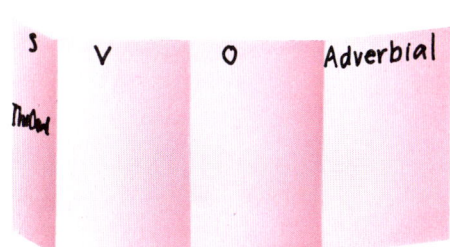

3) Then fold over the paper so that nobody can see what is written in the first section.

S
V
O
Adverbial

4) Now pass the papers clockwise to the next person in the group. On the new paper you have just received write a verb (choose from our list of transitive verbs and write in the present tense), then fold over and pass the paper on again.

5) On your new paper write an object (choose from our examples or make up your own). Then fold over and pass on again.

On your last paper, write an adverbial (choose from our examples or make up your own).

Then fold over the paper and pass it on for the last time. If there are four in the group you will now have your original paper back again.

When everyone is ready, open your papers and read out the sentences you have created – there will probably be some very silly and funny ones.

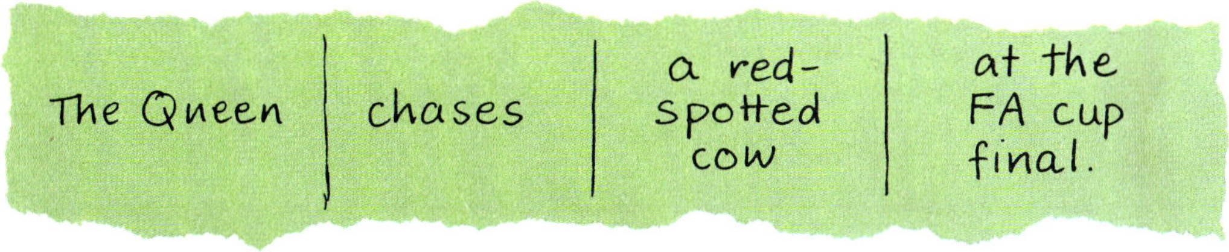

The Queen
chases
a red-spotted cow
at the FA cup final.

**In your language book**

Write the heading: **Subjects, Verbs and Objects**

**A** Copy and complete:

> Every sentence has a s_____ and a v_____. Some sentences also have an o_____. The o_____ can be a person or a thing, which usually has something done to it in the sentence. Not all v_____s take o_____s. O_____s, like s_____s, can be expanded or reduced.

**B** Copy out these sentences, labelling the subject, verb and object with S V O, like this –

$$\begin{array}{ccc} S & V & O \end{array}$$
The dog ate a bone.

1) The gardener pruned the roses.
2) Mrs Beeton wrote a cookery book.
3) In Wonderland, Alice met a white rabbit.
4) To stop the match the referee blew his whistle.
5) Damian threw the ball over the wall.

**C** Expand these sentences by making up nouns or noun phrases for the *objects*, and putting them in place of the pronouns in the original sentences.

1) The policeman caught him.
2) I hate it.
3) Children like them.
4) The army attacked it.
5) The teacher praised her.

**D** Reduce these sentences by replacing the subjects and objects with pronouns.

> 1) Roman men wore togas.
> 2) Queen Elizabeth I knighted Sir Francis Drake on board his ship.
> 3) Later, Sir Francis Drake defeated the Spanish Armada.
> 4) Mr Walt Disney produced cartoon films.
> 5) The person who is writing this sentence is wearing shoes.

(Remember to make the verb agree!)

**E** Using the transitive verbs on page 27, make up three short sentences of your own and write them down, labelling the parts S, V, and O.

31

# 5 Spoken and Written Language: Standard English

Previously in *Mind Your Language* we have looked at some of the important differences between spoken and written English.
List as many of these differences as you can.

There is another great difference between written and spoken English.

Spoken English can *sound* very different, depending on which part of the country or which part of the world the speaker comes from. People have different *accents* and different *dialects* (ways of using words). But written English is the same all over the country – it is known as Standard English.

**Scotland**

D'ye ken whaur Alec is?

Naw I havenae seen him the day, hen.

**Standard English Version:**
Do you know where Alec is?
No, I haven't seen him today, dear.

Choose one or two of these examples and work out *exactly* how the Standard English version is different from the spoken dialect version.

Perhaps there is a dialect (or there may be a number of dialects) in the area where you live. Try to think of examples of how people's speech in your area is different from Standard English.

Sometimes there are special dialect words, which people who do not speak your dialect would not understand.

**Scotland**
baffies – slippers
messages – shopping or errands
lum – chimney

**Lancashire**
butty – sandwich
mither – pester or get on someone's nerves
clemmed – starving, hungry

**London**
plates (of meat) – feet
scarper – run away

**West Indian**
dash down – throw away
palaver – talk, argument, trouble
belly work – stomach trouble

Do you know any dialect words from your area?

One of the most common differences between dialects and Standard English is the different use of the verb "to be". You can see this in one of the examples on page 33. Is the verb "to be" used differently from the standard form in your area?

*The Standard Form of the Verb "To Be"*

PRESENT TENSE

| Singular | Plural |
|---|---|
| I am | We are |
| You are | You are |
| He ⎫ | |
| She ⎬ is | They are |
| It ⎭ | |

PAST TENSE

| Singular | Plural |
|---|---|
| I was | We ____ |
| You ____ | You ____ |
| He ⎫ | |
| She ⎬ ____ | They ____ |
| It ⎭ | |

What are the missing *Standard English* forms?

Here are a few examples of spoken dialect sentences. How would these be written in the Standard English form?

1) I done it yesterday.
2) He ain't got it.
3) It was her what said it.
4) I dinnae ken the way.
5) He don't know much, do he?
6) She were right clever.
7) We was eating – and we was drinking too.

> Some people, like the newsreaders on TV, *speak* in Standard English, as well as writing it. But it would be a very dull world if everyone spoke Standard English all the time and dialects were to die out.
>
> Most people agree, though, that we should all *write* in Standard English. What does *standard* mean? (Check in a dictionary to be sure.)
>
> What advantages are there to having a *standard* written form of the language?

**A Dialect Play**

Work in groups of three to five people. Make up a short play in dialect. It would be best if you could do it in your own local dialect, but if you do not have one, try to use a dialect like Lancashire (*Coronation Street*) or East London (*EastEnders*). Or try Australian English (*Neighbours*).

Don't try to write your play down – writing dialect can be difficult! Perhaps some of the plays can be put on tape, for other classes to hear.

**Slang**

As well as dialect words, spoken English usually includes *SLANG* words and expressions. Slang is a bit like dialect, except that it tends to be associated with a *time* rather than a *place*. Young people at different times often have their own slang words and expressions.

We were having such a jolly evening – topping fun! But then a flapper with a bob gave me a gasper, and – my dear – too, too sick-making!

We had a wizard time barging about the countryside. And then Ginger pranged his old man's old banger, and that was our transport kaput.

It was a groovy scene – way out! – and I really dug it. But we ran out of bread and Mark was feeling grotty, so we split.

1920s    1940s    1960s

Nowadays, these slang expressions seem very out of date, and some of them don't make sense to the modern reader. (Standard English versions can be found on page 66 if you can't work them out.)

Can you think of any modern slang? What words do *you* use, for instance, to say that something is really good? Or really bad? How about words to say you're feeling ill?

**In your language book**

Write the heading: **_Standard English_**

**A** Copy and complete:

> People speak in different ways in different parts of the country. They have different a_____s and d_____s. And different age groups often have their own s_____ words and expressions. But written English should be the same everywhere so that everyone can understand it. It is known as S_____ E_____.

**B** Copy out these sentences, putting *was* or *were* in the spaces to make the Standard English form.

> 1) We _____ late for school.
> 2) You _____ at home last night.
> 3) I _____ very tired.
> 4) He _____ full of energy.
> 5) I _____ not sure where you _____.
> 6) She _____ told that they _____ coming today.

**C** Write out the correct Standard English forms of these sentences:

> 1) I done it this morning.
> 2) She ain't got no idea.
> 3) It were her dad what said it.
> 4) You don't know nothing.
> 5) He didnae ken my name.

**D** Make up three sentences in your own dialect or a dialect you know well and write them down. After each one write the correct Standard English form.

# 6 The Apostrophe to show Ownership

You have already met the apostrophe in Book Two of *Mind Your Language*. It is a punctuation mark that looks like a flying comma, and it appears *inside* words like this:

isn't  he'll
it's  we'd
I've  o'clock

it's

What job is the apostrophe doing in the words above?
How does a writer know exactly *where* the apostrophe should go in each one?

Let some people write on the board the shortened forms (with apostrophes) of the following words:

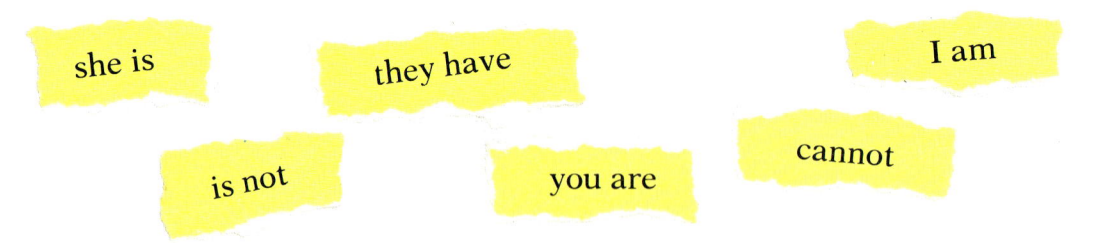

she is    they have    I am
is not    you are    cannot

The apostrophe has another job in English. It shows *ownership*.

Marianne's schoolbag = the schoolbag belonging to Marianne.

In the two phrases above, who is the *owner*?
What part of speech is this word?
What item is *owned*?
What part of speech is this word?

What are the missing words in these pairs of phrases?

David's lunch = the _____ belonging to _____.
Anne's watch = the _____ belonging to _____.
The teacher's temper
             = the _____ belonging to the _____.
The _____'s _____ = the bowl belonging to the dog.
_____'s _____ = the book belonging to Flora.
_____'s _____ = the nose belonging to Sam.

What part of speech is each missing word?

In the following sentences, try substituting a "belonging to" phrase whenever ownership is mentioned, as in this example:

We all watched *Jo's TV*.
We all watched *the TV belonging to Jo*.

> My mum's name is Susan.
>
> The horse's mane is long and silky.
>
> We came to school in Mr Green's car.
>
> The princess kissed the frog's head.
>
> Our dog's tail is shaggy.
>
> There is a book called "Gulliver's Travels".
>
> The teacher marked her pupil's book.

Sometimes the belonging-to phrase sounds a bit silly, but where there is an apostrophe showing ownership you can always substitute it without losing the sense.

In each of the above sentences who is the *owner*? What part of speech are these words?
   In each of the sentences, which is the item which is *owned*? What part of speech are these words?

**Spot the Rule**

Work in pairs. Work out a basic rule for using the apostrophe to show ownership. Make your rule as clear as possible, so that a young child could understand it. Write it down on scrap paper.

   When you have finished, each pair can tell the class their rule, and the class can choose the best version.

**Who owns What?**

Split into four groups. Each group needs a box or tray and a piece of paper. Everyone in the group puts one item that he/she owns into the box. It can be a pencil, an item of clothing, a badge, etc., etc. Each member of the group then signs his/her name on the piece of paper like this:

When all the groups are ready, the boxes and papers are passed clockwise to the next group.

Each group now has the task of matching the items in the box to the owners on the list.

The lists should be completed like this:

*Beth*
*Alistair*
*Imran*

*Beth's pencil*
*Alistair's sock*
*Imran's badge*

When all groups are finished, the boxes and lists are passed back to their owners, who tick or cross the guesses. To score a tick,

1) the owner must be correctly matched with the item
2) the apostrophe + s must have been correctly filled in on the sheet.

The winning group is the one with the best score.

**BEWARE** The apostrophe is one of the most misused punctuation marks. It is needed for two things:

1) to show shortened forms
2) to show ownership (where the owner is a noun).

But some people seem to think that every word ending in "s" needs an apostrophe. They put apostrophes in all over the place. Their written work begins to look as though it's got the measles.

*Lots* of words in English end in "s" and *don't* show shortened forms or ownership. For instance –

The present tense of many verbs – "He *walks* home."
Some adjectives – "the *enormous* house" some pronouns – "*his* desk", "the books are *ours*", "the dog licked *its* bowl".
Many plural nouns which have nothing to do with ownership – "I like *sweets*", "The *dogs* barked".

In the next passage, there are lots of words ending in "s". Tell your teacher what they are, so that he/she can make a list on the board.

> Roald Dahls book *The Twits* is very funny. It is about a couple called Mr and Mrs Twit who play tricks on each other. For instance, Mr Twit puts a frog in Mrs Twits bed. Mrs Twit feeds her husband spaghetti with worms in it.
> It is quite an easy book to read and most children like it. Roald Dahl is the most popular childrens writer these days. His books are always in the Top Ten best sellers.

*Three* of these words need apostrophes before the "s" to show ownership. But most of them are just ordinary words ending in "s".

To check whether a word needs an apostrophe, to show ownership try these tests:

Is it a noun? — NO — no apostrophe
YES ↓
Can you do the "belonging to" substitution? — NO — no apostrophe
YES — apostrophe

Which are the three words in the passage that need an apostrophe before the "s"?

Who is the owner and what is the item owned in each case?

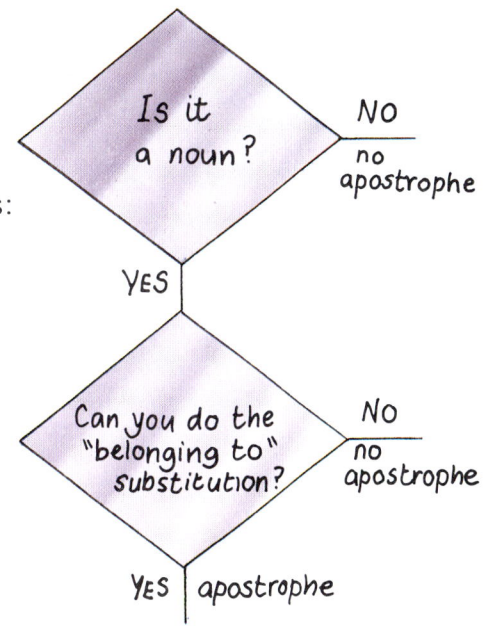

**MAKE SURE YOU USE APOSTROPHES ONLY WHEN YOU NEED THEM. IF IN DOUBT, MISS IT OUT!**

**In your language book**

Write the heading: **Apostrophes to show Ownership**

**A** Copy and complete:

> An ap_____ is a punctuation mark that looks like a flying c_____. It has two main uses:
> 1) in sh_____ forms of words it shows where letters have been m_____ o_____;
> 2) it can show o_____ship. Where a noun is an "owner," you add an ap_____ + s, to show o_____ship.

**B** Copy and complete:

> Matthew's coat — the coat belonging to _____.
> Alexander's drum — the _____ belonging to _____.
> Mum's cup — the _____ belonging to _____.
> The postman's bag — the _____ belonging to _____.
> _____'s _____ — the book belonging to Andy.
> _____'s _____ — the hair belonging to Hannah.
> _____'s _____ — the name belonging to the teacher.

**C** In each of these sentences substitute the "belonging to" phrase with a phrase using an apostrophe to show possession.

> 1) The *armour belonging to the knight* was very heavy.
> 2) We made our way up to *the castle belonging to Count Dracula.*
> 3) *The mane belonging to the lion* was thick and matted.
> 4) *The horse belonging to Dick Turpin* was called Black Bess.
> 5) I picked up *the books belonging to the children.*
> 6) *The child belonging to Monday* is fair of face,
> 7) *The child belonging to Tuesday* is full of grace.

**D** Look through a book to find at least four examples of the apostrophe used to show ownership. Copy out the phrases concerned, and beside each of them write the "belonging to" version.

**E** Copy out this passage and put in apostrophes to show ownership *where they are needed.*

> Many writers have used pen-names to conceal their identity. Samuel Clemens, for instance, wrote books under the name of Mark Twain. Twains books included *Tom Sawyer* and *Huckleberry Finn*. Lewis Carrolls real name was Charles Dodgson – he was a University lecturer who disguised himself to write *Alices Adventures in Wonderland*. And perhaps the most famous of all childrens writers also had a pen-name – Enid Blytons real name was Darryl Waters.

**If You've Managed All That, Read On**....

There is one last point about the apostrophe to show ownership. If the owner-noun already has an "s" at the end, you don't need to add another one. You simply add an apostrophe at the end of the word. For example, the words "James" and "princess" both end in "s":

   The book belonging to James – *James' book*.
   The crown belonging to the princess – *the princess' crown*.

This is most common in the case of regular plural nouns, e.g. horses, girls, dogs, boys.

   The reins belonging to the horses – the *horses'* reins
   The cloakroom belonging to the girls – the *girls'* cloakroom.
   The bowls belonging to the dogs – the *dogs'* bowls.
   The toilet belonging to the boys – the *boys'* toilet.

This helps clear up any confusion about whether the owner is singular or plural. You cannot tell in spoken language, but written language makes it clear:

   The coats belonging to the girl – the girl's coats
   The coats belonging to the girls – the girls' coats.

# 7 Words at Work: Adverbs, Prepositions and Conjunctions

**Adverbs**

An adverb can tell you more about a verb.
Match up these types of adverbs to their names.

tells you where something happens — adverb of time

tells you when something happens — adverb of manner

tells you how something happens — adverb of place

Find the adverb in each of these sentences and say which type it is.

The fire brigade is coming quickly.
The fire brigade is coming here.
The fire brigade is coming now!

*Quickly! Here! Now!*

What type of adverb could each of these words be?

sadly   yesterday   everywhere   primly   here   often

there   loudly   immediately   never   left   right   fast

## Prepositions

Another part of speech is the preposition.
Prepositions are little words which come at the beginning of phrases.
The phrases below all begin with a preposition:

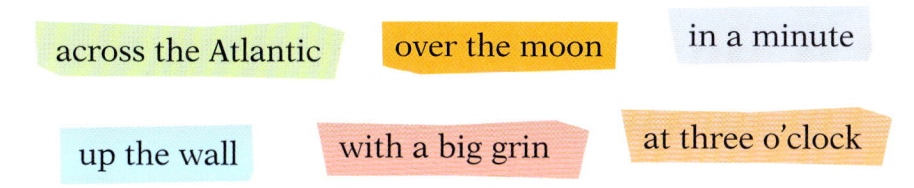

across the Atlantic     over the moon     in a minute

up the wall     with a big grin     at three o'clock

A phrase which starts with a preposition is called a **prepositional phrase**.
What is the preposition in each of the prepositional phrases above?
Use the same prepositions to make up more prepositional phrases.

Prepositional phrases can be very short:

the Prince (of) Wales          a stitch (in) time

or quite long:

The robber always went shopping (in) his favourite stripy jersey and black mask.

Here are some more words that can be used as prepositions:

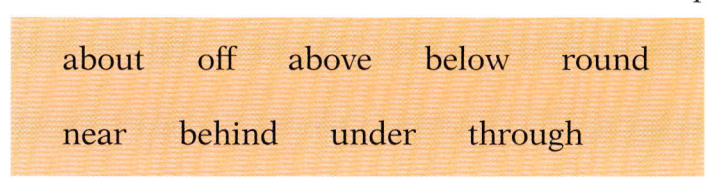

about    off    above    below    round

near    behind    under    through

Think of a prepositional phrase starting with each one.

Prepositional phrases often do the same job in a sentence as adverbs – they tell how, when or where something happens. This is because we often need more detail than can be contained in a single adverb.

Which of the prepositional phrases you have made do an adverbial job, and answer the questions how? when? where?

### Work with a partner

Look through a book or magazine for prepositional phrases. List them under these headings:

| time (when?) | place (where?) | manner (how?) | other |
|---|---|---|---|
|  |  |  |  |

## Prepositions and adverbs

Some words can act as prepositions or as adverbs.

In the pairs of sentences below the same word is being used as
(a) an adverb of place
(b) a preposition at the beginning of a prepositional phrase.

Which word is it each time, and which use is which?

I looked round.
I looked round the corner.

I glanced up.
I glanced up the road.

He jumped off.
He jumped off the cliff.

She fell down.
She fell down the stairs.

**Conjunctions**

Conjunctions are joining words.
Some simple conjunctions can be used to join words

> black *and* white

or phrases:

> all the king's horses *and* all the king's men

or clauses:

> This is a clause *and* this is another clause.

Try joining some words, phrases and clauses with these conjunctions:

> *but*   *or*

Other conjunctions (like **if** and **unless**) show more complicated relationships between ideas. These conjunctions can link clauses together to create complex sentences.

*conjunction*    *main clause*

> *If* Daisy feels hungry, dad rushes to feed her.

*subordinate clause*

*conjunction*

> Daisy is miserable *unless* Rover is around.

*main clause*    *subordinate clause*

47

Here are some more conjunctions:

(when)  (because)  (until)  (although)

How many different complex sentences can you make using
- the four conjunctions above
- the four clauses below.

(Try to make two-clause, three-clause and four-clause sentences.)

King Kong came crashing through the city

everyone fled screaming

buildings were collapsing all around

little Daisy Miller could sleep through anything

Which is the main clause each time? How do you know?

### Work with a partner

You need a long strip of paper, like a roll of left-over wall paper.
Make up a complex sentence containing at least three clauses.
Draft it on scrap paper.
Then write your sentence as one long strip:
- do not put a capital letter at the beginning
- do not put a full stop at the end
- do not go onto a new line at any point.

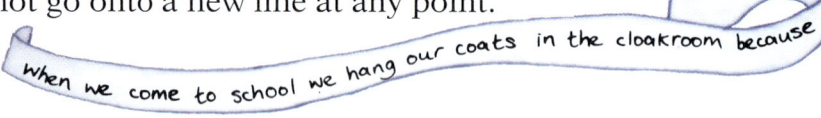

*when we come to school we hang our coats in the cloakroom because*

Cut up your sentence into individual clauses. Cut off the conjunctions separately.

| when | we come to school | we hang our coats in the cloakroom | because |

Can you use the conjunctions to put your sentence together in any other order? Can you think of other conjunctions you could use to put your sentence together?

Swap strips with another pair. Can they put your original complex sentence back together? Try mixing up the other pair's clauses with your own. Can you make any interesting complex sentences?

**In your language book**

Write the heading: *Adverbs*

**A1** Copy and complete:

> An a_____ is a p_____ of sp_____ . It can tell you how, when or where something happens in a sentence. An a_____ of m_____ tells you h_____ something happens. An a_____ of t_____ tells you w_____ something happens. An a_____ of p_____ tells you w_____ something happens.

**B1** Draw three columns, labelled

| adverbs of manner | adverbs of time | adverbs of place |

Write the words from the blue box on page 44 in the correct columns.

**C1** Find all the adverbs in these sentences. Write them in the correct columns in your book:

> 1) Next door's cat often stands outside yowling miserably.
> 2) The schoolchildren rushed excitedly indoors.
> 3) My nephew is always tearing noisily upstairs and downstairs.
> 4) Yesterday I ran home, but today I'm walking steadily.

Write the heading: *Prepositions*

**A2** Copy and complete

> Another p_____ of s_____ is called the pre_____ . The pre_____ is usually found at the beginning of a phr_____. A phr_____ that starts with a pre_____ is called a pre_____ phr_____.

**B2** Make up prepositional phrases beginning with these prepositions:
1) across   2) over   3) in   4) with   5) at   6) to

49

**C2** Put each of the prepositional phrases you made in B2 into a sentence.

**D2** Make up a prepositional phrase to complete each of these sentences:

| | |
|---|---|
| The panther padded silently _____ | (where?) |
| The church clock stopped _____ | (when?) |
| My brother made mud pies _____ | (how?) |

Write the heading: *Conjunctions*

**A3** Copy and complete

A c_____ is a joining word. You can use simple c_____ to join w_____s, phr_____s or cl_____s. Some conjunctions can show more complex relationships between ideas.
　We use these to link cl_____s together to make c_____ s_____s. A c_____ s_____ has one m_____ cl_____ and one or more s_____ cl_____s.

**B3** Choose suitable conjunctions from the box below to join these pairs of clauses into complex sentences.

　　　because　　when　　until　　after

1) the baby cried loudly _____ its mother ran into the room
2) Red Riding Hood was skipping home _____ the wolf jumped out
3) it was cloudy _____ the sun came out
4) the runners were exhausted _____ they had run 26 miles

**C3** Choose one of the pairs of clauses from B3 and find at least 4 different ways of combining them into a complex sentence by
• using different conjunctions
• changing the order of the clauses.

# 8 Inverted Commas

Inverted commas are sometimes called "speech marks" because they are used to show words spoken in direct speech. But they have other uses too.

> My favourite books are "Charlie and the Chocolate Factory" and "Stig of the Dump".
>
> I always watch "Blue Peter" and "Top of the Pops".
>
> We went to the cinema to see "Bambi".
>
> Our school carol service always begins with "Hark, The Herald Angels Sing" and ends with "Oh Come All Ye Faithful".
>
> Three of Shakespeare's most famous plays are "Hamlet", "Macbeth" and "Romeo and Juliet".
>
> I like the poem "Windy Nights" by Robert Louis Stevenson.

There are words in inverted commas in each of the sentences in the box. Go through them one by one and work out what sort of thing has been put in inverted commas in each sentence. What do all these things have in common?

Inverted commas can also show that a writer is writing *about* a word, not using it for its meaning.

**If you're not sure what "inverted" means, look it up in the dictionary.**

The words "telephone", "television" and "telepathy" all come from the Greek word "tele", meaning "distant".

51

Have you noticed any other times that inverted commas are used by writers? Keep an eye open when you are reading and see if you can spot any more uses.

However, the most frequent use of inverted commas is to show direct speech. We looked at direct speech in Book 3 – can you remember what the term means?

The passage opposite from the beginning of a *William* story by Richmal Crompton involves a lot of direct speech. Beside it we have placed the same passage with everything blocked out except the direct speech punctuation.

Read the story silently first. Then your teacher can choose three people to read it out loud – one can be William, one can be his mother and the other can be the narrator.

Then, while your teacher prepares the next section (see page 54), try your hand at detective work.

**Direct Speech Detective Work**

Work with a partner. Use the *William* story and the blocked version to work out the answers to the following questions. You don't need to write anything down.

1) Some of the words have been blocked out in red, and some in blue. What are the red blocks?
2) What are the blue blocks?
3) Which punctuation marks are *always* put around direct speech?
4) Apart from punctuation marks, how does the writer show that one person has finished speaking and another one has started to speak?
5) Where does the full stop go at the end of a piece of direct speech – inside or outside the inverted commas?
6) What punctuation mark is *usually* used instead of a full stop *before a blue block*? Is it inside or outside the inverted commas?
7) When is a question mark used instead of a comma? Is it inside or outside the inverted commas?
8) The writer opens two sections of direct speech without using a capital letter (line 6 and again 3 lines from the end) – try to work out why.

When your teacher is ready, discuss your answers with the rest of the class. How good a detective were you?

# William Goes for a Nice Little Walk

"Why are you doin' all this muddlin' about?" said William, throwing an interested glance round the disordered room.

"I'm spring cleaning, dear," said Mrs. Brown, "and get out of the way."

"But it's not spring," objected William. "You can't do spring cleanin' when it's not spring."

"I know it's not spring, dear, but I had 'flu in the spring and had to put it off. Now *do* get out of the way."

"Well, I don't mind helpin' a bit with spring cleanin'," said William, his interest increasing as he inspected the chaos that surrounded him. "I did help last year, didn't I?"

"If you call it helping," said Mrs. Brown, plunging the vacuum cleaner attachment into the recesses of the settee. "You scrubbed your father's chair, loose cover and all, and left it *sodden*. Dripping with water right through to the floor. He was furious. He couldn't use it for weeks."

"Well, it was clean," said William after a moment's thought. "An' I'm a year older than that now. I've got a good bit more sense than I had all that time ago. An' anyway it was a *sens'ble* thing to do. That water goin' right through cleaned the inside. I bet you'd've only cleaned the outside, your way. I bet that chair's never been so clean in its life as what it was when I'd finished with it."

"Even after it was dry it gave your father lumbago.... Do leave the vacuum alone, William."

"I was only wonderin' how it worked.... Well, what can I do to help?"

"You can go away," said Mrs. Brown. "You can go for a nice little walk."

"Oh, all right," said William distantly, "if you don't *want* me to help ... but I bet I *could* help all right."

Your teacher can choose people to come out and punctuate this passage correctly.

Excuse me said Charlie to the man standing next to him at the bus stop you have a newt on your shoulder
Yes I know said the man its my pet
Oh said Charlie does it have a name
Yes replied the man I call it Tiny
Why do you call it Tiny asked Charlie
I should have thought that was obvious said the man I call it Tiny because its my newt

**In your language book**

Write the heading: **Inverted Commas**

**A** Copy and complete:

> In_____ c_____s are used to show d_____ speech. They are placed around the words actually spoken. Any punctuation which goes with the d_____ speech is included *inside* the in_____ c_____s. A c_____ is usually used to separate the direct speech from the rest of the sentence (unless a qu_____ m_____ or ex_____ m_____ is required).
>
> In_____ c_____s can also be used around the titles of books, films, etc., and around words which are being discussed in a piece of writing.

**B** Each of these sentences contains a title. Work out which words are part of the title and write out the sentences, putting in capital letters and inverted commas where necessary.

1) Betsy Byars is an American authoress whose books include the eighteenth emergency and the midnight fox.
2) The Walt Disney film one hundred and one dalmatians has a villainess called Cruella De Ville.
3) Bob Geldof wrote a song called do they know it's christmas to help the starving people of Africa.
4) My mum and dad argue because she wants to watch sports grandstand and he wants to watch the film on the other channel.

**C** Find a story book with plenty of direct speech in it. Choose a passage to copy out – about half a page long. Copy it, but change all the writing to blocks, as we have done with the *William* story on page 53. Use red blocking for direct speech and blue blocking for the rest. Show all the punctuation clearly.

**D** The comic strip below tells a short story about Biffo and Buster. Write this story *in words* in your language book, using direct speech techniques to present the words in the speech bubbles. Make sure your punctuation is perfect!

# 9 Words and Meaning: Idioms

*This sum is hard.*

*My ice-cream is hard.*

*My sum is harder than your ice-cream.*

*Don't be silly.*

What is silly about what the boy said in the last picture?

Jill's hair is long.
My library book is long.
My library book is longer than Jill's hair.

Beth caught a cold.
Beth caught a netball.
Beth caught a cold and a netball.

Jamie took his library ticket.
Jamie took his time.
Jamie took his library ticket and his time.

There are some things you *can* say in English, and some things you *can't* say.

In each of the three examples above, the first two sentences are fine, but most people would agree that the last sentence is silly. In each case, try to explain why.

When we are talking English we don't often stop to consider exactly what we are saying. We know how to use words to make sense, and we do it without thinking. People from foreign countries are often baffled by the English language. They do not know what you can and cannot do with words, so they often make mistakes.

They are also often baffled by *idioms*. Idioms are ways of saying things. In an idiom the meaning of the saying really has nothing to do with the meaning of the words used.

The police, working under cover, caught the thief red-handed.

This sentence means that the police (who were working in disguise) caught the thief while he was in the act of committing a crime. Nobody was actually under a cover and nobody actually had red hands.

What do these idioms mean?

1) He has *green fingers*.
2) The teacher *let the cat out of the bag*.
3) I am trying *to kill two birds with one stone*.
4) She gave me *the cold shoulder*.

These pictures are silly illustrations of some well-known idioms. Can you work out what they are?

Answers on page 69.

### Idiotic Idioms

Think of any idioms you know – get your teacher to write them up on the blackboard. Choose one of them to illustrate like the examples on page 58.

If you draw your picture on thin card or strong paper, you can cut a flap in an appropriate part of the picture that will lift up. You can then stick a piece of paper underneath the flap with the idiom written on it. People can lift the flap to check what the idiom is.

Mount your idioms on the wall and have a competition to see who can guess the most.

Of course, other countries have their own ways of using words too. Although people in the USA speak English, they often use different words and expressions from those used in Great Britain. We call such words and expressions "Americanisms", and you've probably heard lots of them on American TV shows.

Do you know the British equivalents of these Americanisms?

(Answers are on page 69.)

1) step on the gas
2) the sidewalk
3) the trunk of a car, the fender of a car
4) first grade in school
5) trash cans
6) the school yard
7) Tell that to the Marines
8) ice-box
9) I'll take a rain-check.

An old lady opened the front door and found a tramp standing there in his tatty old clothes and battered hat. He said, "Lord luv yer, Lady, I 'aven't 'ad a bite all day."
So she bit him.

Traveller: Can you give me a room and a bath?

Hotel clerk: I can give you a room, sir. But you'll have to bath yourself.

# 10 Active and Passive Sentences

Read this SVO sentence:

     **S**     **V**        **O**
The Queen ate a jam sandwich.

What is the subject of the sentence?
What is the verb?
What is the object?

You can change this sentence around so that the object becomes the subject:

     **S**         **V**
The jam sandwich was eaten by the Queen.   *Adverbial*

Try changing these sentences round in the same way:

> Koala bears eat leaves.
> West Bromwich Albion won the match.
> The Romans invaded Britain.
> Children watch television.

What happens to the verb when you change a sentence round like this?
    What other little word (a preposition) do you have to add to the sentence each time?

**Active and passive sentences**

All SVO sentences can be turned back-to-front in this way. The original SVO sentence is called an **active** sentence and the verb is an **active** verb.

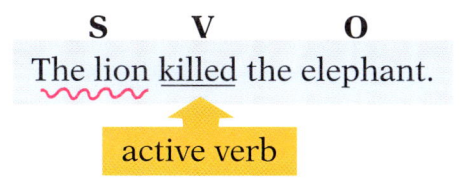

$$\text{S} \quad \text{V} \quad \text{O}$$
The lion killed the elephant.

active verb

The new version is called a **passive** sentence and the verb is a **passive** verb.

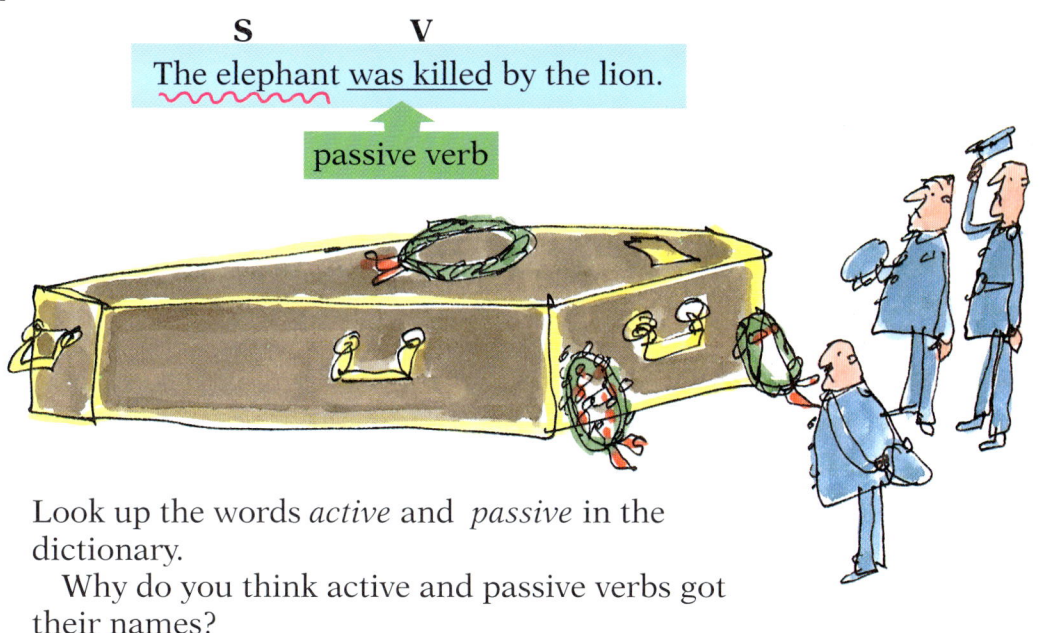

$$\text{S} \quad \text{V}$$
The elephant was killed by the lion.

passive verb

Look up the words *active* and *passive* in the dictionary.
    Why do you think active and passive verbs got their names?

Work with a partner. Divide a sheet of paper into two sections, labelled ACTIVE and PASSIVE.
    Think of three active SVO sentences to write in the ACTIVE section. Then convert them into passive sentences in the PASSIVE section.

| ACTIVE | PASSIVE |
|---|---|
| We love Maths. | Maths is loved by us. |

**Who dunnit?**

When a sentence changes from active to passive, the subject changes too.

      S      V      O            S      V
The pirate buried the treasure. ⟶ The treasure was buried by the pirate.

    ACTIVE                 PASSIVE

Change this active sentence into the passive.

      S      V      O
The dog discovered the treasure.

What is the subject of your passive sentence?

In a passive sentence, the subject doesn't actually do anything.
**It has something done to it.**
   Sometimes a writer may not want to say **who** was responsible for an action. On these occasions, writers often use passive sentences and miss off the final phrase.

The treasure was buried.            by the pirate.

The treasure was discovered.        by the dog.

Maybe the writer **doesn't know** who was actually responsible for a particular action.

> The jewels were stolen.
> A present was left on my doorstep.
> The lock on the filing cabinet has been broken.

Or maybe the writer **prefers not to mention** who was responsible.

Change these sentences into the passive. Then take off the final phrase so that the reader doesn't know who was responsible for each action.

> I broke the vase.
> James destroyed the flowerbed.
> My friends and I ate my sister's birthday cake.

> Remember:
> If you don't want to mention "who dunnit", use a passive sentence!

## Impersonal writing

Passive sentences are often used in scientific writing. When scientists write up an experiment, they have to explain everything very clearly, so that other scientists can copy the experiment in exactly the same way. This means there must be
- all information necessary to repeat the experiment
- no unnecessary detail
- no mention of the person who is doing the experiment.

Passive sentences are perfect for this sort of **impersonal writing**.

| Personal style | Impersonal style |
|---|---|
| I put the seed in direct sunlight. Then I watered it whenever the soil was dry to the touch. | The seed was placed in direct sunlight. It was watered whenever the soil was dry to the touch. |

Make these sentences **impersonal** by
- changing them into the passive
- removing the reference to the person or people who did the work.

> James and I planted the seed in sandy soil.
> Mr Roberts held the stick in place with a lump of plasticine.
> The children pushed the egg into the milk bottle.
> The school pig took away the cap and tie.

Two-clause sentences can be passive too.
Make these sentences **impersonal**:

> We placed the second lot of seeds in the sunlight but we did not water them.
>
> We placed the frogs in the tank and left them for 2 days.
>
> The school pig took away the cap and tie and destroyed them.

**In your language book**

Write the heading: *Active and Passive Sentences*

**A** Copy and complete:

> Every simple sentence has a s_____ and a v_____. Some sentences also have an o_____.
>
> An SVO sentence is called an a_____ sentence and the verb is an a_____ verb.
>
> If you change an SVO sentence round so that the o_____ becomes the s_____ it is known as a p_____ sentence and the verb is a p_____ verb.
>
> P_____ sentences are often used in imp_____ writing such as science reports.

**B** Change these sentences from the active to the passive. You will have to:
- change the form of the verb
- add the preposition "by".

> 1) Constable Nabb caught the burglar.
> 2) Isaac Newton discovered gravity.
> 3) The Romans conquered Britain.
> 4) The teacher marked the books.

**C** Make these sentences more impersonal by:
- changing them into the passive
- missing out all references to the people who did the experiments.

> 1) Richard and I placed the magnet under a sheet of plain white paper.
> 2) Richard shook some iron filings on to the paper.
> 3) I directed the beam of light on to the prism.
> 4) The children of class 6A collected the results and displayed them in a table.

**D** Find three examples of the use of the passive in non-fiction books and copy them into your language book.

**Standard English Versions** for page 36

1920s  We were having such a pleasant evening – great fun! But then a smart young woman with short hair gave me a cigarette, and – my dear – it made me feel very sick.

1940s  We had a marvellous time rushing about the countryside. And then Ginger crashed his father's old car, and that was out transport gone.

1960s  It was a very enjoyable place to be – very special – and I really enjoyed it. But we ran out of money and Mark was feeling off-colour, so we left.

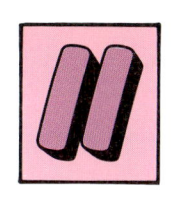

# Sorts of Sentences and Sentence Transformations

We can talk about sentences in terms of the job they do.

### Statements

Most sentences are straightforward statements of fact. But they can be *positive* or *negative*.

YES

NO

Which of the words in the speech bubbles above would you call positive and which negative?

1) Mandy likes ice-cream.   2) Mandy does not like ice-cream.

Which of the above sentences is positive and which negative? What do you think *negative* means?

Change these sentences into the negative by adding *one word*:

1) I am the best runner in the class.
2) My name is Archibald.
3) London is in Wales.

These sentences need a little more changing to become negative.

1) The dinosaur ate the plants.
2) Boris plays tennis.

What exactly did you have to do in each case to make the sentence negative?

Change these sentences into the positive:

1) Wimbledon is not a tennis tournament.
2) The Queen of England did not sit on the throne.
3) I don't like maths.

## Questions

You can make statements into *questions* by turning them round a little:

↳ Rhet likes ice-cream.
↳ Does Rhet like ice-cream?

↳ The cat was brown and fluffy.
↳ Was the cat brown and fluffy?

> 1) Henry VIII had six wives.
> 2) The larch is a coniferous tree.
> 3) Christmas Day is on 25th December.
> 4) It's a long way to Tipperary.

What sort of things do you have to do to the sentence when you make it into a question? Turn the sentences above into questions.

## Commands

Another special sort of sentence is the *command*.

Please hurry up.   Put your coat on.   Eat your custard!   Close that door!

What is the verb in each of the above sentences?
What is the subject?

> In commands we say that the subject is *understood* – that is, we know who it is, but we don't mention it in the sentence. And the subject is always *you* (the second person singular or plural) – that is, the person or people being told what to do. Who's the subject in these commands?

Look!

Drink your milk.

Put that book down and go to bed.

Give that to me, please.

For each of the sentences in the box below, say –
   a) whether it's a statement, a question or a command;
   b) whether it's positive or negative;
   c) what the verb is.
Does punctuation help you to decide sometimes? If so, how?

1) The dog was fast asleep.
2) The dog wasn't fast asleep.
3) Was the dog fast asleep?
4) Wasn't the dog fast asleep?
5) Go to bed!
6) Don't eat that!
7) Did the Ancient Britons paint themselves blue?
8) Eat up your spinach like a good boy.
9) It's not fair!

The explanatory sentences in this chapter are all statements, questions or commands. Look back over the chapter and find a couple of examples of each.

**Answers (page 58)**

1) done up like a dog's dinner
2) cool as a cucumber
3) over the moon
4) words on the tip of your tongue
5) full of beans
6) keep your nose to the grindstone
7) a lame duck

**Answers (page 59)**

1) go faster
2) the pavement
3) the boot of a car, the bumper of a car
4) first year infants
5) rubbish bins
6) school playground
7) I don't believe you. (Pull the other leg.)
8) refrigerator
9) I'll come another time.

**Using the Rules: Sentence Transformation**

In the four books of *Mind Your Language* we have been looking at spoken and written English, and learning a little about how language – especially written language – works.

But before you started work on *Mind Your Language*, even before you started school, you already knew a great deal about how language works. You had worked it out for yourself without really noticing, by listening to adults talking and sorting out the rules in your head. The proof of this is that you learned to talk.

Learning to talk is a very special human skill. The rules of language are so complicated that, so far, only human beings have managed to learn them. Nobody has yet been able to program a computer to "speak" without human help. When you learned to talk as a little toddler, you were proving yourself cleverer than any computer in the world!

Take a simple SVO sentence like "The girl wore jeans." Inside your head are all the rules you need to change that sentence in lots of ways:

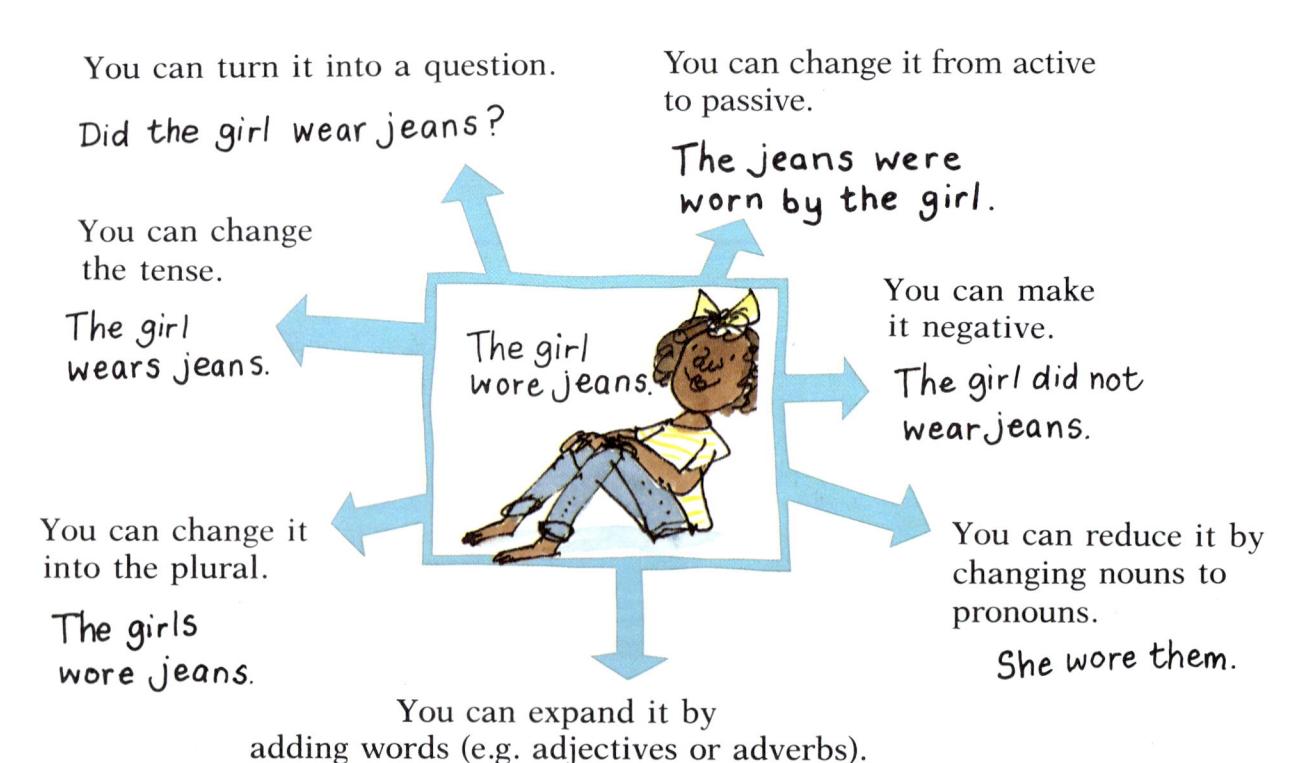

You can turn it into a question.

*Did the girl wear jeans?*

You can change it from active to passive.

*The jeans were worn by the girl.*

You can change the tense.

*The girl wears jeans.*

*The girl wore jeans.*

You can make it negative.

*The girl did not wear jeans.*

You can change it into the plural.

*The girls wore jeans.*

You can reduce it by changing nouns to pronouns.

*She wore them.*

You can expand it by adding words (e.g. adjectives or adverbs).

*The tall dark girl wore patched old jeans.*

You can do all these things and many more without really thinking about it.

Aren't you clever?

Try doing the same things to this simple SVO statement.

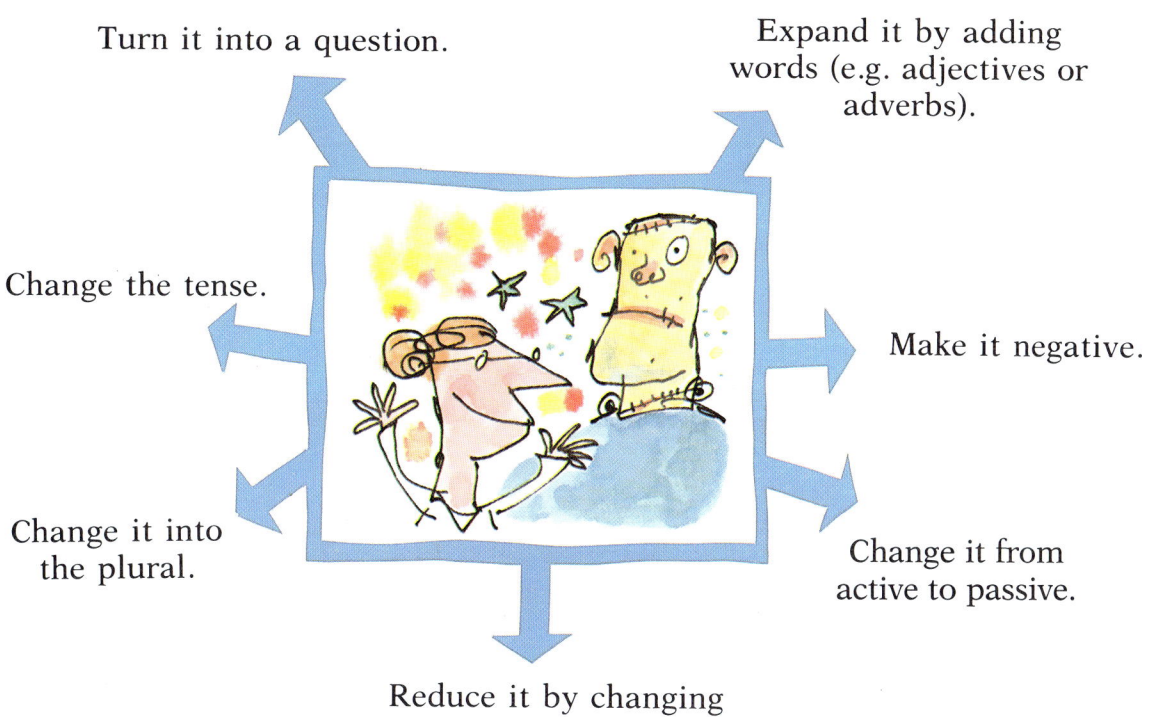

## The scientist made a monster.

Turn it into a question.

Expand it by adding words (e.g. adjectives or adverbs).

Change the tense.

Make it negative.

Change it into the plural.

Change it from active to passive.

Reduce it by changing nouns to pronouns.

### Messing about with a Sentence

Work in pairs. Make up your own short sentence – a *positive statement* (SVO is best). Do the seven changes that we have done above.

When you are satisfied that your work is correct, make a small poster, set out like our example in the box on page 70, with your sentence in the middle and the changed versions around the outside.

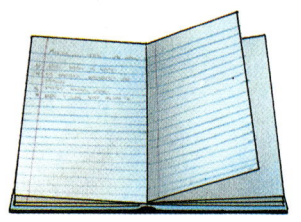

**In your language book**

Write the heading: *Sentences*

**A** Copy and complete:

> We can describe sentences in terms of the jobs they do. A sentence that tells you something is called a s_____. It can be p_____ or n_____. A sentence can also be a qu_____ or a c_____ (In c_____s the subject is u_____).

**B** For each of the sentences below, state whether it is:
  a) a statement, a question or a command,
  b) positive or negative.
The first one is done for you to show you how to set it out.

> 1) Don't do that!
>    a) command   b) negative
>
> 2) London stands on the River Thames.
> 3) Did the First World War start in 1914?
> 4) Didn't the First World War start in 1914?
> 5) Come and see me.
> 6) Don't knock that lamp over!
> 7) I am thirteen years old.
> 8) Doesn't Angie look smart?
> 9) Aren't you cold?
> 10) Write your name along the dotted line.

**C** Change the following statements into questions:

> 1) Jamie is older than you.
> 2) He is really frightened.
> 3) Tadpoles turn into frogs.
> 4) The Great Fire of London started in Pudding Lane.
> 5) Transitive verbs can take an object.

**D** Make up a short SVO sentence. Now make the *seven* changes listed on page 71 to your sentence – write down the seven new sentences.